Our King Lives

The Pursuit of our Lord and Savior Jesus Christ

Organized and Authored by Mike Gillard

To the lost, the defiled, the godless so that all might
believe in The Only Begotten Son our Lord

Jesus Christ

Contents

Prelude

With the expansion of moral ambiguity, secularization of institutions, and production of totalitarian policy, there seems to be adequate evidence that western civilization is being restructured into an execrable society that leads to the pinnacle of anguish. Therefore, the average can no longer stand by as our nations and families are plunged into darkness. The time has come to make a stand to restore our hearts which will restore our nation. The core question that we should ask ourselves is, "Where do we begin"?

Teaching the average man that the best dream that you can have is how to establish a personal relationship with Jesus Christ. After a relationship is established, the focus should be on perfecting your relationship with Jesus. As men set their house in order by driving out sin, women will begin to do the same as we are all called to contribute and return to our father's house. Therefore the content within this literary work is not only orientated at driving people to faith in Jesus Christ, but also on how to perfect that faith, and how to realign our churches.

Through truthful speech and strong Christian leadership, the true potential of nations can be fully realized if we are willing to take upon ourselves the cross that is in front of us. We have an obligation to speak the truth and have a relationship with the truth. Jesus Christ is the truth.

Society is being primed for a biblical Christian revival, therefore this work is written in advance to assist all those who are willing to learn of the optimal way to establish a relationship with Jesus.

There is a way to save civilization, and his name is Jesus Christ.

Note:

This literary work has not been created to replace scripture or supplement it. These are simply thoughts and conclusions whether they are right, wrong, complete, or incomplete.

Dreams and False Tactics

The well-meaning pursuit that many of us have is to define a dream and work to pursue it by all means necessary. As our lives progress, we tend to iterate upon our original dream to ensure that we meet some kind of fulfillment. In our pursuit, we may have the chance to understand that the dreams in which we have defined are inwardly seeking, worldly, and based in deception. To provide some examples, many dreams that many follow are as such:

1. Wealth
2. Intelligence
3. Happiness

As we continue to develop and pursue false dreams, the more hell manifests itself in our everyday life. The Bible tells us in Revelation 9:2 King James Version that hell is a bottomless pit. This is due to deception and sin. The more we trust deception and embody worldly dreams, the more we descend into hell. The Bible also tells us in Psalm 9:17 KJV that the sinners are turned into hell. This clearly articulates to us that as we pursue deception through sin, our lives become infinitely worse. Remember that God our father is in heaven, therefore hell is the inverse of heaven. This equates that our primary dream is to pursue Jesus Christ and deny the world and all the false pursuits that it provides.

When defining a future state of existence or a dream, there is **one** dream with **three** dimensions that equates to everlasting life in this world and in heaven:

To find and be worthy of Jesus Christ's eternal presence

1. The Way in which we choose throughout our lives
2. The Truth that we have a relationship with
3. The Life that we acquire as a result of pursuing and finding Jesus Christ

The rationale for why this dream is ideal is because it is a tangible and verifiable expression of how we can bring eternal life into our current and eternal existence.

When we pursue The Way, we begin to drive sin out of our life while they develop their relationship with God's word. If you have a relationship with The Bible, you have a relationship with Jesus because in John 1:14 KJV it states that Jesus Christ is the word made flesh.

By finding and loving the truth, you can resolve problems

weapon against the enemy. This
10:34 KJV that he did not
word. As you embody the
ble to resolve your own
problems that destroy the
why the truth does not always
kes men confront the way
that they change. This is why
ss. In John 3:19 KJV it explains
kness rather than light because
ou begin to speak truth, you will
enemy of the world, but of
s in Galatians 4:16 KJV, "Am I
emy, because I tell you the

The life that we acquire as a result of our pursuit and discovery of Jesus Christ is the perfect happiness and peace that so many seek by following deceptive worldly dreams. Christians are at complete peace because they have come to the shared understanding within God's church that our father is in control and has a plan for each and every person. Some would say that it is naïve, but those that say this have not searched and have not found what they are looking for.

Just as there are false dreams, there are false tactics on how we can replace God. Here are some examples of false tactics that ultimately lead us away from Jesus Christ even though it can appear to be a just pursuit:

1. Believing in yourself, that you are enough to fix your own problems
2. To do more good works than evil works, that you might be worthy of salvation
3. To become as God, that you may be equally powerful and all knowing

The narrative from the world is that we should believe in ourselves. As if when we believe enough in ourselves, that we can achieve anything we want. This is not only pure narcissism, but idolatry that is condemned by The Ten Commandments. We shouldn't believe in ourselves, mankind, or any politician. What happens when you are not enough, or mankind is not enough, or a politician is not enough? Your life plunges into chaos as a result of not having a stable foundation. Our sole focus should be on Jesus Christ. As a result of believing in him, your life will radically improve.

The only way to wash away your sins is to accept Jesus Christ as the messiah who gave his life so that we can all live with him forever. The rationale here is if you sin, you will die in your sins as we read in John 8:24 KJV. Good works will never cancel out our sins. You cannot negotiate with God and justify your sins by doing good deeds. Either you follow him entirely without reservation or you don't follow him at all. There is no middle ground and you cannot negotiate middle ground due to your good deeds. You cannot serve two masters; you must pick Jesus over The Devil.

There seems to be a belief that if we as a society advance technologically, we can be God and understand how such power and authority can be utilized for man's wicked use. The Devil has tried to be as God and failed. What makes us think that we are smarter or more capable than an angel who was in the presence of God when the world was made? God will only reveal himself to those that are pure in heart and worthy of his presence.

Hopefully you have come to the realization that The Devil is very real. That his deceptions are real and his evil is expressed throughout our world. There will always be another lie that he will produce that will drive The Planet Earth, what was supposed to be a paradise, into a state of constant pain and misery. There is an answer to this evil, and his name is Jesus Christ.

As you continue reading, you will understand how Jesus can change you, the world, and how you can develop a better relationship with Jesus Christ by means of changing your heart to align with biblical truth.

Tactics and Concepts for Perfecting Your Relationship with Jesus Christ

#1 Know Christ like the Centurion

In John 3:16 KJV we learn that belief in Jesus Christ is what is required to never die and to achieve eternal life. What if there is something stronger than solely believing? After much thought and practice, it has been made clear that belief itself is not a finite point. Moreover, belief seems to be the minimum requirement for salvation. Belief seems to be the beginning point in which we can give our hearts through faith to reach a higher state of understanding Jesus, which seems to be more accurately articulated as "Knowing" Jesus Christ. As a result of this ascension toward Christ, your sins seem to die from your heart and you completely transform as an individual. When the Centurion came to Jesus in Matthew 8:5-13 KJV, he asks for Jesus to heal his servant. He does not need to see the miracle and he pleads that Jesus does not come to his house as he is not worthy. He seems to know without reservation that Jesus Christ is King. Therefore, his servant is healed just as Jesus speaks. When we know that Jesus is King, what miracles could come into being within our own lives? "Be still, and know that I am God; I will be exalted among the nations, I will be exalted in the earth!" (Psalm 46:10 KJV).

The only way to increase your faith from simple belief to knowing Jesus is to hear the word of God as we read in Romans 10:17 KJV. Many people hear the word and turn from it because they are unwilling to open their hearts to him. "And this is the condemnation, that light is come into the world, and men loved darkness rather than light, because their deeds were evil." (John 3:19 KJV).

Therefore, when we hear the word of God, we must embody it into our hearts so that we might make our lives and the world around us a better place. When people are unwilling to accept the blood of the lamb on their hearts, the destroyer will take you for all eternity. God tells Hosea the prophet in 4:6 KJV, "My people are destroyed for lack of knowledge". Every man belongs to Jesus Christ regardless of your sins, demographic, and current belief. You are worth fighting for because God himself determined at the beginning that he would make you in his image. In Isaiah 46:10 KJV we are able to understand that God declares the end from the beginning and his purpose will stand. In Jeremiah 1:5 KJV God says, "Before I formed thee in the belly I knew thee…" Jesus Christ loves you not only today, but also for your potential.

Always remember that you have a choice. Turn to him and repent of your sins and he will begin to open your eyes to his divine plan. You must accept him or you will die in your sins not just for one day, but for all eternity. Hell is a prison and so terrible that not even The Devil and his angels want to go there. Hell was designed for The Devil and his angels and not for us. Therefore it is our duty to commit our hearts to Jesus and learn to believe so that we may live forever. Jesus Christ calls us by name through the darkness of this world.

#2 Jesus' Two Commandments

Jesus gave us two commandments in Matthew 22:37-40 KJV that are the foundation of all other commandments, laws, and the prophets.

1. Thou shalt love the Lord thy God with all thy heart, and with all thy soul, and with all thy mind.
2. Thou shalt love thy neighbor as thyself.

When we embody these two commandments, the following then becomes instantiated in our lives:

1. The Ten Commandments
2. The Seven Laws of Noah
3. The Law of Moses
4. Strength and conviction of the Prophets
5. Manifestation of the holy spirit by means of spoken truth

As we integrate Jesus' two commandments into our hearts, the truth itself begins to grow within our heart. This growth seems to not only change our lives, but the other laws given to the prophets seem to also become manifest in our lives. Here are some examples:

1. If you love God completely, you begin to stop following Idols like money or other false dreams per The Ten Commandments.
2. When you love your neighbor as yourself, the salvation of others becomes an important focus in your life. This is the inspiration for why saints and prophets are willing to give their lives for the purpose of evangelism. **Losing even one person**

to everlasting damnation is one person too many.

3.   When you completely surrender to the cross, there seems to be a life changing event that disassociates your concerns from the world and connects your concerns to Jesus. How do I make a difference? How do I save more people?

When Abraham took his son Isaac to the mountaintop in Genesis 22 KJV as a sacrifice to The Lord, an angel of The Lord stopped him from sacrificing his son. Abraham said that God will provide his only son instead, the perfect lamb. When we accept Jesus Christ as Lord and as The Lamb of God sacrificed from the foundation of the world, we won't have to sacrifice anything because Jesus Christ is the lamb that was sacrificed on our behalf. Through faith, we can all be worthy of God's presence.

#3 How to Pray

God's word tells us to pray always in 1 Thessalonians 5:16-18 KJV. However, how do we pray always and the correct way? We can take a look into some of the greatest biblical heroes to understand the correct way to pray. There are three focuses that we must keep in consideration when praying.

1. Your Soul
2. Your Heart
3. Your Mind

When you pray, you are focusing all that you are out to The Lord. The potential ever present communion with Jesus Christ is the focus that we must remember when seeking him. The connection with Jesus Christ is something that can happen at all times even when we are asleep. An important thing to note here is that you have to want it with all your heart. You will never be tempted into a relationship with Jesus; you have to break through the temptations of this world to find him.

King David commanded his soul to praise the living king in Psalm 43:5 KJV. David recognized his soul as a separate element of his being that he has control over. He commanded his eternal soul to worship God. This satisfies the first part of Jesus' first commandment.

The second element of effective prayer is a little bit more complicated. The prophet Daniel would face the temple in Jerusalem and open a window when he prayed that faced toward the holy city and holy temple. He would physically orientate his heart toward where God's presence was. Due to the indwelling of The Holy Spirit given in The New Testament, God does not dwell in temples of stone but temples of flesh as we read in Acts 7:48-49 KJV and 1 Corinthians 3:16 KJV. This means that we must focus on the presence of Jesus Christ in our hearts instead of a temple in Jerusalem when we pray. One other scripture that provides light on this subject is Jeremiah 29:13 KJV, "You will seek me and find me when you seek me with all your heart."

The final part of prayer is to ensure that our minds are filled with God's word. The only way for the impossible to be accomplished is to embody God's word in our minds by study of The Bible and then to act upon it. The reason why this is so important in prayer is that as you study the word, it begins to dominate your thoughts. Then your mission as a result of prayer becomes very clear. A perfect example would be Ezra and Nehemiah. Both of these two men committed themselves to God and his word through prayer and study of The Old Testament. Then their mission to rebuild Jerusalem's communities and walls became clear as a result of this commitment.

As we pray, always give thanks to Jesus Christ first before asking of anything that you need. Ensure that as you pray, you do not ask for money or things that belong to the world. Ensure that you ask for a new heart, a new life, and a new direction so that you may be filled with God's great purpose. Prayer is one of our weapons against the world because "For every one that asketh receiveth; and he that seeketh findeth; and to him that knocketh it shall be opened." (Matthew 7:8 KJV). Just ensure that you are praying for the right things, the things that God wants you to pray for. Never stop fighting the good fight of faith and prayer shows God that we still are fighting this fight.

#4 Born Again

When Nicodemus came to Jesus, he knew that the father had sent Jesus. Jesus replied and told him, "Verily, verily, I say unto thee, Except a man be born again, he cannot see the kingdom of God." (John 3:1-3 KJV). Nicodemus was a religious leader, but religious practice is not enough to save you. No amount of religious traditions or service can save you! Jesus looked at the Pharisees in Matthew 21:31-32 KJV and said "The publicans and harlots go into the kingdom of God before you". This is because they know they need a savior to take their sins. Only faith in Jesus Christ has the power to save you. Good works that lead people to Jesus are not enough to be saved for all eternity. Even religious leaders must have faith to enter into Heaven as we read in Ephesians 2:8-9 KJV, "For by grace are ye saved through faith; and that not of yourselves: it is the gift of God: Not of works, lest any man should boast."

What does it mean to be born again? This means that every single person has to recommit themselves to Jesus Christ the Lamb of God. It is by the blood of the lamb by which man is saved. How often must be commit ourselves to him? Within Numbers 28:3 KJV we learn that the Lord told Moses that The Children of Israel must sacrifice a lamb without blemish in the morning and evening every day. Jesus Christ is the perfect Lamb of God that was sacrificed on the cross so that we might live with him forever. Therefore, we must recommit our hearts to Jesus Christ twice a day, in the morning and the evening.

Do not gamble with your soul. You have no idea when your last day on this earth will be, therefore you must get your heart right with God now! Do not wait until you're older to come to Christ, do not wait until you have more money, or a more "successful" life. Jesus Christ will give you everything that you need and he will guide you through this life.

There are many claims that press the idea that once we are saved, we are always saved. This is a lie! You must continue to renew your relationship with God by means of giving your heart to him, by being born again. You can lose your salvation if you reject Jesus Christ at any time. That emptiness that you may feel now is only the beginning of what death feels like. You can fill the emptiness that you feel in your heart the moment you come to Jesus Christ. Do not let your pride keep your soul out of the kingdom of Heaven. There is nothing from this world that you should lose heaven for! Come to Jesus Christ now from this day and forever.

Jesus said "For whosoever will save his life shall lose it: and whosoever will lose his life for my sake shall find it." (Matthew 16:25 KJV). You must deny your current lifestyle and let it die from you. When you deny yourself and pick up your cross to follow Jesus you will have life everlasting. Part of being born again is denying your current heart and accepting the new heart that Jesus Christ is offering you. As a result of being born again, the cross in front of you becomes clear. Take it and follow Jesus Christ.

The last point with regards to being born again is specific to seasons. Everything from a biblical perspective happens in seasons of time. There is a season of renewal, a season of persecution, a season of exile, a season of sickness, a season of revival. Regardless of what season you are going through right now; always remember to pray and to give your heart to Jesus Christ at least twice every day.

#5 World vs Jesus

When Jesus was in the desert in Matthew 4:1-11 KJV, The Devil manifested himself to Jesus and tempted him in three ways.

1. To satisfy his hunger by turning stones into bread
2. To jump off the pinnacle of the temple so that Jesus' angels would save him
3. To gain the whole world in exchange for worshipping The Devil himself

Today through the entertainment industry, our secular institutions, and through the media, it is quite clear that they tempt us away from God. The world seems to have a propensity to encourage the satisfaction of our earthly desires whether it is consumption of food, drink, sex, wealth, fame, etc. The important concept to note here is that desire by itself is not a bad thing; however we must guide it to desire the right things. Through faith in our Lord we can drive our desire to love one another, rebuild relationships and communities, and to seek out the word of The Lord. If you are being tempted into an action, this is not from God as we know that God will never tempt you. We as Christians must reject temptation and seek out that which our Lord provides us.

As we plunge into nihilism at the direction of the world, we begin to feel overcome with worthlessness and self-pity at the idea of our own existence. Many people will begin to ask themselves, "Why was I created to suffer?" and "Does my life have any meaning in the midst of all this suffering?" This will ultimately lead to a deceptive solution to remedy our painful existence by means of suicide. The ammunition that drives so many people to suicide and despair is deception itself that manifests through the media, our institutions, and the entertainment industry. The infrastructure to disseminate deception was created long ago and hijacked by The Devil himself to make our lives unlivable. He hates us and wants every moment of our existence to be in infinite pain and perversion to spite our Lord. You mean so much to Jesus that he created and died for you. That being said, we have an obligation to fight against deception in our world so that we may find the peace and paradise that was designed for everyone. We fight by having a relationship with Jesus Christ, prayer, and speaking the truth each and every day.

The Devil offered the whole world in exchange for Jesus' worship. Jesus denied The Devil. One verse that offers us some insight is Matthew 16:26 KJV when Jesus says "For what is a man profited, if he shall gain the whole world yet loses his own soul? Or what shall a man give in exchange for his soul?" Those who are willing to give their soul to The Devil can become wealthy, famous, and have what they think they need. However, these things will lead to eternal damnation. Never gamble with your soul; you have no idea when your last day will be. If you don't believe that The Devil dominates the world, look at the statistics regarding the amount of porn watched each day on the internet, the tattoos, satanic symbolism, and the amount of deception used in the political structures around the world. The Devil dominates the world for now, but soon the kingdoms of the world shall be thrown down and become the kingdoms of our Lord. (Revelation 11:15 KJV).

Remember what Jesus said in John 15:19 KJV, "If you were of the world, the world would love its own. Yet because you are not of the world, but I chose you out of the world, therefore the world hates you." When we as Christians accept Jesus and embody The Holy Spirit in our hearts, the world will begin to harshly judge us. The world said of John the Baptist that he was possessed. (Matthew 11:18 KJV). Jesus said of John the Baptist that this is the greatest man and greatest prophet to have lived. That is what the world will always do, mischaracterize and judge wrongly. The world accused Jesus of being gluttonous and a winebibber or what we would today call a drunk. Again, this is an expression of what is wrong with the world. It is so far from God that even 2000 years later we can realize that so little has changed.

#6 Repentance

Western society in which we live has been inundated with the narrative that we should do as we please. The narrative that we have been fed from an early age is to do whatever seems to be convenient, sounds nice, or feels right. 1 John 3:4 KJV, "Whosoever committeth sin transgresseth also the law: for sin is the transgression of the law." When we sin, it is an act of lawlessness against the orderly laws that God has given us to live out our lives in the full potential in which it was designed. His laws are designed to protect us so that we were not deprived of the goodness of his gifts. Due to this lawlessness, we are separated from God. Therefore, to pursue our Lord we must drive sin out of our lives.

In the aftermath of sin, we have an opportunity to repent and return to God. However, we live in a society where sin is taught, celebrated, and institutionalized. As Isaiah the prophet said, "Woe unto them that call evil good, and good evil; that put darkness for light, and light for darkness; that put bitter for sweet, and sweet for bitter!" (Isaiah 5:20 KJV). When we mischaracterize the definition of good or create our own values as a society, we begin the painful plunge into darkness that has the capacity to destroy nations. When Ezekiel laid on his side for 365 days on the Jerusalem wall warning judgement was coming because of their sins, they did not repent. (Ezekiel 4 KJV). Exactly one year from the beginning of his prophecy, the city of Jerusalem was destroyed by Nebuchadnezzar II of Babylon. And God said," A third part of thee shall die with the pestilence, and with famine shall they be consumed in the midst of thee: and a third part shall fall by the sword round about thee; and I will scatter a third part into all the winds, and I will draw out a sword after them." (Ezekiel

5:12 KJV). Sin has a very high price if we choose not to turn from it and repent.

However, we have a choice to make. Repent and return to God, or continue on this path of self-destruction. **DO NOT BE A SLAVE TO THE DARKNESS!** For King David wrote in Psalm 9:17 KJV, "The wicked shall be turned into hell, and all the nations that forget God." In Acts 3:19 KJV, it makes clear what appropriate actions we can take, "Repent ye therefore, and be converted, that your sins may be blotted out, when the times of refreshing shall come from the presence of the Lord." We can usher in a season of renewal if we choose to repent and return back to God. This is especially relative to wildfires, sexual confusion, political anger, and distrust of media.

"And I will make the land desolate, because they have committed a trespass, saith the Lord God." (Ezekiel 15:8 KJV). Through apostasy, sinful actions, and poor legislative decisions, America is being turned into Hell. The proof is quite clear if we look at California; its homelessness, drug addiction, wildfires, and poverty. "If my people, which are called by my name, shall humble themselves, and pray, and seek my face, and turn from their wicked ways; then will I hear from heaven, and will forgive their sin, and will heal their land." (2 Chronicles 7:14 KJV). The solution here is quite clear.

No amount of government, global warming policy, or man-made values will ever save us. These false narratives will ensure that America descends into hell. Hell is a bottomless pit because there is always another lie to descend us further away from God. Per this descent, the individual and nations will bear more pain and suffering as a result. There is only one truth, one way to save us, and one author of our salvation. His name is Jesus Christ.

#7 Temple of the Living God

Jesus Christ lives in our hearts. "Ye are of God, little children, and have overcome them: because greater is he that is in you, than he that is in the world." (1 John 4:4 KJV). Therefore, we have an obligation to not treat our bodies as a tool for entertainment, but a place worthy of the presence of Jesus Christ. This exactly why being drunk, high, pursuing extramarital satisfaction, premarital sexual satisfaction, or manipulation of our physical body is a sin against God. It defiles that which God made and desires to live in.

As it says in Proverbs 31 KJV," Give strong drink unto him that is ready to perish, and wine unto those that be of heavy hearts." It appears here that alcohol in moderation of acceptable, but those who over consume should be ready to deal with the consequences. Where everyone needs to proceed with some degree of caution is that alcohol can be a doorway to anger, addiction, and anguish. You always have to defend yourself against The Devil and his legion because they will continue to find a way to attack your heart. One sin always will lead to another which opens your heart to more anguish. It appears that when your heart is lost, your mind soon follows. For example in Mark 5 KJV, when Jesus arrived in the country of Gadarenes, he encountered a disturbed man on the shore of the sea. This man spent time loitering in cemeteries and tombs as if lost hearts likes places of death like deserts and cemeteries. This man also cut himself, proceeded to have unnatural strength enough to break chains because of his rage, and spoke with a strange voice. A man completely depraved of all the good things that God gives us. When this man encountered Jesus Christ, the legion inside him spoke for him and cried "...My name is Legion: for we are many." Mark 5:9 KJV. You see that when one spiritual entity gains hold of your heart, it tries to open other doors for other tormenting spirits as the scripture calls them. This is exactly why we must not determine one sinful behavior as acceptable as it will lead to another and we will end up being in a constant state anguish and depravity.

In today's world, there are quite a few practices that focus on what God has made for the purpose of perversion. Remember that only God can create life. The Devil is unable to create life. Therefore out of spite, he will always try to pervert God's creations and twist his words to bring his chaotic evil world into existence. There are some practices that already exist and a few that are soon to exist in our world that drive the sanctity of God's creation out of the human race, and they are as follows:

1.   Cosmetic surgery
2.   Tattoos
3.   Piercing other than ears
4.   DNA Editing
5.   Integration of Technology into the body

The purpose of cosmetic surgery, tattoos, and excessive piercings is fundamentally to improve your image. Whether it manifests itself as appearing younger, being lighter weight, more in style, or more sexually attractive. The only type of alteration that is acceptable biblically is to pierce your ear lobe on each side. (Deuteronomy 15:17 KJV). The Law of Moses makes it clear that for servants of a household both men and women are to pierce their earlobes as a sign of servitude. **Make certain that you do not wear any demonic symbol on your ears as it shows**

who you serve. In today's world, we do not have servants that serve a family like we had in The Old Testament; however it provides some insight into what are the limitations for piercings. Our Lord has made you the way you are for a reason and you are most certainly famous and loved in his eyes. You should not feel a need to alter yourself whether it is for popularity, shock value, or a partner. Although it is very enticing that we could easily modify ourselves to improve our image, this is not the biblical way to improve our image. "So God created man in His own image; in the image of God He created him; male and female He created them." (Genesis 1:27 KJV). We have already been created in the image of God and we don't need to make changes that would pervert that image.

With regards to DNA editing or integration of technology into the body, which is a form of transhumanism, these things are not acceptable in God's eyes. There was a time in The Bible where DNA of humankind became altered. This was a time during and prior to the time of Noah which was part of the reason for the flood. "And it came to pass, when men began to multiply on the face of the earth, and daughters were born unto them, that the **sons of God saw the daughters of men** that they were fair; and they **took them wives** of all which they chose. And the Lord said, My spirit shall not always strive with man, for that he also is flesh: yet his days shall be an hundred and twenty years. There were giants in the earth in those days; and also after that, when the sons of God came in unto the daughters of men, and they **bare children** to them, the same became mighty men which were of old, men of renown. And God saw that the wickedness of man was great in the earth, and that every imagination of the thoughts of his heart was only evil continually." (Genesis 6:1-5 KJV). "Sons of God" is a term used in The Old Testament and the beginning of The New Testament to describe the father of a given person. For example, if your dad's name is Aaron, you would be described as a son or daughter of Aaron. There are only two biblical individuals and one group of beings that are described as the sons of God:

1. Adam who was directly created by God the Father. (Luke 3:38 KJV). Adam would be described as a Son of God from an Old Testament and early New Testament perspective.
2. Jesus Christ who is God and his father is God due to the virgin conception and birth. (Luke 1:34-35 KJV).
3. The Angels created directly by God. (Genesis 6 KJV).

"And when her days to be delivered were fulfilled, behold, there were twins in her womb. And the first came out red, all over like an hairy garment; and they called his name Esau. " (Genesis 25:24-25 KJV). How can a newborn baby be full of red hair like he was wearing a sweater? Could this be the caveman DNA that the modern day scientists have found? Was Esau a giant? Esau's descendants are known as Edomites. Edom means red in Hebrew. God hated Esau, Malachi 1:3 KJV, "And I hated Esau, and laid his mountains and his heritage waste for the dragons of the wilderness."

We know from 2 Peter 2:4-5 KJV that God sent the angels that took women for themselves to a place called Tartarus. In the original Greek, hell is described as a bottomless pit. However there are three sections of hell that are specifically called out in Greek and they are as follows:

1. Hades/She'ol – Waiting place of the dead in Christ and the dead away from Christ. Those here are awaiting either the rapture of the church or judgement. (Ecclesiastes 9:2-3 KJV).
2. Gahenna – The burning pit also known as the lake of fire. (Matthew 5:22-29 KJV).
3. Tartarus – A place worse than Gahenna, the lake of fire. This place is actually far deeper into Hell than Gahenna. What is worse than Tartarus? Something to think about. (2 Peter 2:4 KJV).

As a result of reading all of this, let's sum it up very briefly:

- Angels can manifest themselves as physical beings.
- Angels took women and had offspring known as Giants or Nephilim.
- The DNA of mankind seems to be different in the Old Testament days if we look at Esau as an example.
- God judged the angels that took women for themselves and sent them to Tartarus.
- God sent a flood to cleanse the earth while saving Noah and his family.

During the time of Noah, he spent decades building the Ark. Noah knew full well that a flood would come and take all the sinners away. In Genesis 6:9 KJV, "These are the generations of Noah: Noah was a just man and perfect in his generations, and Noah walked with God." The word for perfect in Hebrew is Tamiym, which means without blemish, undefiled, and perfect. We know in Revelation 13:16-17 KJV that technology will soon exist that allows you to buy and sell seems to be integrated into the human race known as The Mark of The Beast. If you want to be perfect like Noah, do not change your DNA, or integrate technology into your body. Turn from your sin and believe in Jesus Christ.

You are probably wondering what this has to do with Jesus Christ. Jesus says in Matthew 24 KJV, "But as the days of Noah were, so shall also the coming of the son of man be." Remember that during Noah's day, sin was everywhere and what it meant to be human changed for many people. When we begin to modify DNA and integrate technology into our physical bodies, it would appear that that The Second Coming of Jesus Christ is near.

#8 Pursue truth over Religious Practice

Jesus was very critical of many of the religious practices of his day. Within The Gospel of Matthew, eight critiques of the Pharisees were provided. They all can be simplified into one perspective. The Pharisees did not love God, embody his spirit into their hearts, and did not reject the world and its temptations. Due to this open rebellion, they will not enter the kingdom of God. This is precisely why Jesus tells Nicodemus that he must be born again. Being a religious leader isn't enough to enter the kingdom of God.

In today's churches, we have the same parallel with Jesus' time. Here are some thoughts to think about that parallel the Pharisees:

1. That you must be at church on Sunday to get to heaven
2. Integration of political viewpoints into the churches
3. Judgmental church leadership and church attendees
4. Church becoming more about life advice then learning to have a relationship with Jesus
5. Churches overemphasizing financial donations

It appears that many of the churches of today's world have completely lost their footing. Remember that salvation is a gift from our Lord and to enter the kingdom of heaven, you must accept Jesus Christ into your heart. As it says in Ephesians 2:8-9 KJV, "For by grace are ye saved through faith; and that not of yourselves: it is the gift of God: Not of works, lest any man should boast." It is not enough to simply identify as Christian or go to church on Sunday.

You have to completely give your heart to Jesus Christ. Believe in him and let him live in your heart. He will completely change your life, it's his promise.

If you are in church and worry about the message, whether the message is true or not there is a solution. The Bible tells us exactly what to do. "God forbid: yea, let God be true, but every man a liar; as it is written, That thou mightest be justified in thy sayings, and mightest overcome when thou art judged." (Romans 3:4 KJV). The idea here is that if you are concerned about messaging, turn to God's word to determine right from wrong. We know for a fact that many leaders whether they are political or spiritual claim to have all the solutions to the world's problems. They suggest that all of these problems can be solved with a quick press of a button or through common sense. They push the narrative that they can usher in a utopian empire if we only support them. The only utopia that we will have on earth is when Jesus Christ sets up his 1000 year millennial kingdom.

Remember that even though we have differences within our Christian denominations, Jesus Christ calls us all by name and he will not divide his sheepfold based upon denominations. As it says in John 10:16 KJV, "And other sheep I have, which are not of this fold: them also I must bring, and they shall hear my voice; and there shall be one fold, and one shepherd." Therefore as a result of such a passage, our call is to work together to save as many people for Jesus Christ and his kingdom as possible. All are God's people.

#9 Acting on our faith

When Jesus was ascending into heaven he told his twelve apostles, "Go ye therefore, and teach all nations, baptizing them in the name of the Father, and of the Son, and of the Holy Ghost: Teaching them to observe all things whatsoever I have commanded you: and, lo, I am with you always, even unto the end of the world. Amen." (Matthew 28:19-20 KJV). Due to the integration of Jesus Christ's presence into our hearts, our responsibility begins to shift into preaching The Word of God to all people. This means those who are willing and already have a relationship with Jesus Christ and those who do not. It is not enough for people to get into heaven through baptism, good works, or simply saying that they are Christian. They must have an active and ongoing relationship with Jesus Christ. The best way to win people for Jesus Christ is to preach the truth as we read in Romans 10:17 KJV, "So then faith cometh by hearing, and hearing by the word of God."

You can begin to make an impact in our world. This impact is directly tied to your faith. ""Truly I say to you, whoever says to this mountain, 'Be taken up and cast into the sea,' and does not doubt in his heart, but believes that what he says is going to happen, it will be granted him." (Mark 11:23 KJV). You cannot have doubt as it contradicts your faith. With strong enough faith you can bring hundreds, thousands, and even millions to Jesus Christ. "Jesus said unto him, If thou canst believe, all things are possible to him that believeth." (Mark 9:23 KJV). A good question to ask oneself is, "To what degree of faith is required so that we can do that which is required of us?"

A great starting point is to continually pursue the source of truth being Jesus Christ. From there, take upon yourself more responsibility than you can bear. As a result of doing this, your heart will change, your responsibility will align itself to Jesus Christ, and the world around you will improve radically. Preach The Gospel of Jesus Christ in the streets, schools, prisons, media, for the purpose of giving everyone the opportunity to make a decision.

God holds back his final judgement until every single person makes a decision. Either you choose Jesus Christ, or you choose the world and its false gods. "For my name's sake will I defer mine anger, and for my praise will I refrain for thee, that I cut thee not off." (Isaiah 48:9 KJV). In the story of Lot, there are those who love God which is Lot and his family and those who do not. There is no middle ground, no one left uncertain. Then our Lord sent his angels to bring Lot and his family out of Sodom before it was destroyed. All of this is found in Genesis 18-19 KJV. This is a foreshadowing of what is to come in the future. "And the stars of heaven shall fall, and the powers that are in heaven shall be shaken. And then shall they see the Son of man coming in the clouds with great power and glory. And then shall he send his angels, and shall gather together his elect from the four winds, from the uttermost part of the earth to the uttermost part of heaven." (Mark 13:25-27 KJV). The stars of heaven are God's holy angels and the elect are the true Christians who have given their hearts to Jesus Christ. We know that the Elect are true Christians as it explains in Titus 1:1 KJV. This is exactly why evangelism is so important; everyone needs to make a decision as to whether they accept Jesus Christ or the world. No one can be left uncertain.

#10 Pendularity

Throughout the political movements of history, there seems to be a pendulum like effect with regards to the orientation, destination, and reversal of political momentum. Experientially, mankind has endured since time immemorial that political momentum either moves radically right or left until a point is reached in which the political pendulum swings the other way. It appears that the driving force behind such momentum is to build a better nation with less suffering. However, when people acquire an emotional understanding of the end state harm of such momentum, there seems to be a reversal.

Currently as we drive through 2020, the momentum appears to be driving toward a global nihilistic ambiguous orientation. However this seems to only be a transition state at the far left of the pendulum swing that will usher in what is biblically predicted. The Bible tells us of a great Christian revival which appears to be the inflection point in which the pendulum swings to the political right and hopefully not too far. "Jesus replied, "To be sure, Elijah comes and will restore all things." (Matthew 17:11 KJV). This revival seems to usher in the restoration of family values and faith based legislation. After this revival, there seems to be a far right swing of the pendulum according to the scripture appears to usher in a Nimrod 2.0 world leader with a false religious system. **Hijacking of Christianity, but by whom**? By study of the scripture, we can understand the nations that will be involved and how this evil empire will originate. However first, we must understand what criteria must be true before the pendulum swings to the political right:

1. The shared understanding that Jesus Christ is the messiah
2. The empirical evidence that God is real
3. The commonly held narrative that we must legislate that which God has commanded via biblical principles

Once these three criteria are fulfilled, the underpinnings of the final global power will be established. From the prophecy of Daniel 2:31-44 KJV, we understand that four nations other than Israel that will control all of The Holy Land from the time of Daniel until the creation of Jesus Christ's 1000 year kingdom.

1. Head of gold – Babylon
2. Breast and arms of silver – Media Persia
3. Belly and Thighs of brass – Greek Empire
4. **Legs** of Iron and feet of iron and clay – Roman Empire (Constantinople and/or Rome)

Notice that over thousands of year of Israel's history that all of The Holy Land has only been conquered and controlled by empires from the above geographical regions. Based upon the prophecies of The Bible, we are able to understand which nation will control The Holy Land before the return of our Lord. "And it was given unto him to make war with the saints, and to overcome them: and power was given him over all kindreds, and tongues, and nations." (Revelation 13:7 KJV). Based upon this scripture it would appear that the final empire to rule over The Holy Land other than the Jewish people would be an empire with a globalist orientation. We know from the prophecies of the scripture that The Final World Leader will be:

1. Micah 5:5 KJV, "And this man shall be the peace, when the Assyrian shall come into our land: and when he shall tread in our palaces, then shall we raise against him seven shepherds, and eight principal men."

    a. If you read the whole passage, Micah prophesies in The Old Testament days that a savior will be born in Bethlehem. We know him to be Jesus Christ. It will take Jesus Christ to defeat the Assyrian through speech. (Isaiah 30:30-31 KJV).

2. Daniel 9:26 KJV, "And after threescore and two weeks shall Messiah be cut off, but not for himself: and the people of the prince that shall come shall destroy the city and the sanctuary; and the end thereof shall be with a flood, and unto the end of the war desolations are determined."

    a. We know that it was The Romans that destroyed The Holy Temple in Jerusalem in 70 AD. This was The Roman Empire however, which **leg** of The Roman Empire? Was it Assyrian conscripts with direction from Caesar in Rome?

3. In the original Hebrew of Daniel 11:37-39 KJV, the Antichrist will defile The Holy Temple and exalt himself above everything except the god of fortresses. A god that his fathers did not know.

4. He will make a peace deal with Israel for seven years and break it half way though. (Daniel 9:27 KJV).

5. He will be extremely charismatic, attractive, and deadly.

6. Revelation 13:16 KJV," And he causeth all, both small and great, rich and poor, free and bond, to receive a mark in their right hand, or in their foreheads: And

that no man might buy or sell, save he that had the mark, or the name of the beast, or the number of his name."

    a.   If you take this mark, you will never get into Heaven. It is ultimate rejection of Almighty God. Even if they say you can remove it later or it's invisible. You must be ready to die for your faith in Jesus, **DO NOT TAKE THIS MARK**.

The rationale for why so much tribulation shall occur is because it is written in Hosea 5:15 KJV, "in their affliction they will seek me early". At times, we have to be persecuted and drowning in anguish to recognize that we need a savior. We have an obligation to prepare for persecution, may God help us.

Therefore we have an obligation to align ourselves to Jesus Christ our Lord and Savior and ensure that the values in which he has given us are driven to the utmost level. What happens when the Pendularity orientates itself to Christian values with our just king Jesus Christ? This is the utopia that politicians have tried to establish. Instead of rationality and emotionality driving policy, policy will and should be driven by faith. This idea is the underpinning for the kingdom that will never pass away.

#11 Fighting Against the Enemy

The enemy that we fight against is a fallen angel named Lucifer. Lucifer is a Cherubim. Cherubs are the angels that guard The Throne of God. This angel was in the presence of God, denied him, and tried to exalt himself above God. As a result, Satan fell like lightning from heaven as we read in Luke 10:18 KJV. Jesus Christ said of The Devil, "...He was a murderer from the beginning, and abode not in the truth, because there is no truth in him. When he speaketh a lie, he speaketh of his own: for he is a liar, and the father of it." (John 8:44 KJV).

The enemy is Lucifer, who rejects God. Satan's power is manifest through lies. "Be sober, be vigilant; because your adversary The Devil, as a roaring lion, walketh about, seeking whom he may devour:" (1 Peter 5:8 KJV). Lions will often find and stalk weak prey to devour, but sometimes they will go after large and powerful pray as a show of strength and wit. This is how The Devil hunts his victims. Not only does he go after the low hanging fruit being those who do not know Jesus Christ, he tries to take the most faithful people and turn them away from God. **Your heart is his target.**

Paul wrote to The Ephesians the strategy by which you can defend yourself from The Devil and his works. Within Ephesians 6 KJV, we are told to "Put on the whole armour of God." Here are the parts of the armor of God and the meaning:

1.   Loins girt about with truth

Your waist is the center of gravity for your body. It helps you balance as you live out your everyday life. The truth does the exact same thing. The truth helps you not fall away from God and ensures that you live out your life to the fullest potential that God gives you. The truth also pulls you in spiritually, as gravity pulls on us physically each day. You must be willing to seek, embody, and speak the truth.

2.   Breastplate of righteousness

You must learn to conduct yourself ethically through the law given to us by the prophets and by Jesus Christ. The Bible provides us rules by which we govern our lives so that we may be free from sin and its impact on our lives.

3.   Feet shod with preparation of The Gospel of peace

You must be ready to travel for the glory of Jesus Christ. Be prepared to defend God's word, and bring The Gospel of peace to those who have not accepted him.

4.   Shield of faith

This is the most important piece of spiritual armor. Without faith, you will never be able to defend yourself against The Devil. Your faith must be maintained and improved each and every day. Prayer and being born again is what the shield of faith is all about.

5.   Helmet of salvation

You must know how you are saved for eternity. The blood of Jesus Christ that was shed on the Cross, his sacrifice is what makes us free. When you believe that Jesus Christ is The Son of God, who was crucified at Calvary to die for our sins, then you shall be saved.

6.   Sword of the spirit

When you know The Word of God, you can utilize it to deal with problems that arise in your life. You can begin to see the deceptions that have captivated the world. The words of eternal life are never to be underestimated.

#12 Death and Life are Eternal

As we go about our daily lives, we are often distracted by the lures of the world and not focused on what truly matters. Everything that the world offers us is temporary except one thing, death. Therefore we should avoid the pursuits of the world and pursue Jesus Christ for it is written, "Do not love the world or the things in the world. If anyone loves the world, the love of the Father is not in him." (1 John 2:15 KJV). This is why John the Baptist and Elijah spent time praying in the wilderness. The world is corrupted and whether they willingly go into the wild, or are forced to flee, there is a peace and communion with God that can be found there.

Everyone has to make a decision. What do you pursue? Do you follow Jesus Christ or the world? Only through Jesus Christ can you find the fulfillment that you seek. Your heart thirsts for fulfillment. You will never find fulfillment in money, sex, drugs, fame, or political power. "And Jesus said to them, "I am the bread of life. He who comes to Me shall never hunger, and he who believes in Me shall never thirst." (John 6:35 KJV).

When we pursue life itself, we find Jesus Christ at its source. Just as Abraham searched for a city whose architect was God, you find what you seek. For it is written, "For every one that asketh receiveth; and he that seeketh findeth; and to him that knocketh it shall be opened." (Matthew 7:8 KJV). To seek properly, you must give your heart to Jesus and continue the search whether it takes days, months, or years.

We are called by God to make a decision. You must make a decision whether you belong to Jesus Christ or the world.

No one can be in the middle. He holds back his hand of judgement for the perfect hour. For it is written, "The Lord knoweth how to deliver the godly out of temptations, and to reserve the unjust unto the day of judgment to be punished:" (2 Peter 2:9 KJV). You must make your decision, believe or belong to the world. You will have all eternity to remember the choice that you made. To those who chose Jesus Christ, I look forward to seeing you in The Kingdom of Heaven.

We Christians must be ready to give everything for the cross. The world will hate us. They will even kill us, however it is written, "For whosoever will save his life shall lose it: and whosoever will lose his life for my sake shall find it." (Matthew 16:25 KJV).

Hell was designed to be a prison for The Devil and his angels. We do not belong there, we belong to Jesus Christ. Jesus Christ is currently preparing a place for us. "In my Father's house are many mansions: if it were not so, I would have told you. I go to prepare a place for you. And if I go and prepare a place for you, I will come again, and receive you unto myself; that where I am, there ye may be also." (John 14:2-3 KJV).

As our hearts drift from God, doorways open and harmful potential becomes realized throughout our lives and therefore our community. We tell ourselves and friends that we are happier as we fulfill the temptations and lawlessness. However, we are in more pain than before we started to sin and drift from God. There is no life without truth.

Notice that during such drift, convenience seems to be the driving force behind our decision making. What sounds good, what feels right, what is beneficial to our reputation. During such convenience seeking activity, we completely lose Jesus. Notice how it descends on you when you are distant from God and turns your decisions to be impulsive and ensures that you will not be taking into consideration all variables and impacts. Also, convenience is many times inconsistent, can't be measured, and can pervert the very orderly systems for the purpose of finding a shred of fulfillment based in deception.

As almighty God sees your distance and acts, you will reach a point in which he gives your mind over to inconvenience. "And even as they did not like to retain God in their knowledge, God gave them over to a reprobate mind, to do those things which are not convenient;." (Romans 1:28 KJV). Such a distance is not only malignant, but contagious to others. Those who are driven to be fulfilled through inconvenient desires seem to go out of their way to do evil and drive others away from Christ. Even if it takes significant effort, the evil drives them through the inconvenience of their efforts. Notice how inconvenience seems to have no bottom, no end. Just as hell is a bottomless pit.

The last state of a man is one that justifies evil and even calls it good. One that allows himself to be consumed by death and his own works that are not of God. Evil will protect itself with more lies. It will trap itself in your heart, your mind, and be in your eternal presence unless you accept Jesus. When God sees that you are incapable of being saved due to a twisted sense of right and wrong, his final judgement is therefore poured out. This is the last state of a man.

Dream established and Tactics Understood, now what?

When the average man rejects the world and accepts the dream to find and be worthy of Jesus Christ's eternal presence, there is a transformation within his heart that changes the direction of his life. While adopting the tactics of the greatest biblical heroes, it provides each man a capacity to bring a far better world into being and a defense against deception. The core enemy is deception itself being The Devil and his legion. "For we wrestle not against flesh and blood, but against principalities, against powers, against the rulers of the darkness of this world, against spiritual wickedness in high places. Wherefore take unto you the whole armour of God, that ye may be able to withstand in the evil day, and having done all, to stand." (Ephesians 6:12-13 KJV).

As part of the pursuit and embodiment of our Lord, we have an obligation to align our responsibilities away from the world and to him. "Take my yoke upon you and learn from me, for I am gentle and humble in heart, and you will find rest for your souls." (Matthew 11:29 KJV). Every single person has the capacity to bring into being a far better self and world. However, there is only one way, one truth, and one life in which this is to be done. We cannot take steps backward; we must continue to move forward with our commitment to Jesus Christ. The problems of the world are our responsibility and our call to resolve. This is not an easy path, nor is it a noble path in the eyes of the world.

When Jesus Christ was in the desert, he was tempted many times. The Devil has the capacity to give you the whole world in exchange for your soul. "Again, The Devil took him to a very high mountain and showed him all the kingdoms of the world and their splendor. "All this I will give you," he said, "if you will bow down and worship me."" (Matthew 4:8-9 KJV). Nothing of the world will give you the joy and peace your heart so desires. Even though following The Devil seems easier and is tempting, our call is to reject the desires of the world and follow our Lord. "For what is a man profited, if he shall gain the whole world, and lose his own soul? or what shall a man give in exchange for his soul?" (Matthew 16:26 KJV).

Every single person is worth fighting for. Every single person has so much potential to make the world a far better place. However, first you must get your heart right with God. We as individuals and societies must prioritize truthful speech over agenda, over wealth, and over pride. The pursuit of having a relationship with the truth, embodiment of it, and the evangelization of the truth should be the instantiation of our goal.

Just as almighty God split the sea for the Israelites, he will make a way for you. As a result of such, we are called to light a way for him by means of preaching the truth to each and every person. "...Prepare ye the way of the Lord, make his paths straight." (Mark 1:3 KJV). Remember that we will go before him one day, "For it is written, As I live, saith the Lord, every knee shall bow to me, and every tongue shall confess to God." (Romans 14:11 KJV). What words shall be spoken in that day? What words of ours shall be worthy of his presence? Every tongue shall confess in that day that Jesus Christ is Lord. The best and worst people of all of history will bow in his presence and confess. The sad part is that many will come before the Lord and finally understand the value of his love and peace, yet they will be told "Depart from me ye that work iniquity" because they did not reject the world and accept Jesus. Asking for mercy in that day will be too late. (Matthew 7:21-23 KJV).

Prophecies Recently Fulfilled

There are two types of prophecy that are evident in the scripture. The first being prophecy of pattern and the second being revelation. If you can understand patterns in The Bible, you can accurately predict upcoming events. Revelation is the word directly given by God to an individual. There are quite a few prophecies that Jesus spoke of in the scripture that are being fulfilled during this very moment. Here are some of them with thoughts:

- Childless Women
    a. "For, behold, the days are coming, in the which they shall say, Blessed are the barren, and the wombs that never bare, and the paps which never gave suck." (Luke 23:29 KJV).
    b. Notice how in today's world that Men and Women are discussing not having children due to Climate Change. They are even thought of highly or "Blessed" among other couples who decide to have children.
- Walking after Lusts
    a. "Knowing this first, that there shall come in the last days scoffers, walking after their own lusts..." (2 Peter 3:3 KJV).
    b. Today we have Gay and Straight Pride parades. People literally walking after their sexual desires.
- Wars and Rumors of Wars
    a. "And ye shall hear of wars and rumours of wars: see that ye be not troubled: for all

these things must come to pass, but the end is not yet." (Matthew 24:6 KJV).

    b.   The war on women, war on drugs, trade wars, war on men, war on gender equality, war on poverty, etc.

- Ethnic Groups and Earthquakes

    a.   "For nation shall rise against nation, and kingdom against kingdom: and there shall be famines, and pestilences, and earthquakes, in divers places." (Matthew 24:7 KJV).

    b.   In the Greek Bible, which the English was translated from, the Greek word used is," ἔθνος", which is pronounced Ethnos.

Ethnos means Ethnic Group. Therefore, Matthew 24:7 KJV can be interpreted as, "For ethnic group shall rise against ethnic group, and kingdom against kingdom: and there shall be famines, and pestilences, and earthquakes, in divers places."

    c.   Notice how earthquake frequency and location seem to be increasingly normal around the globe. What will happen to California in the near future?

- Easily Offended Generation

    a.   "And then shall many be offended, and shall betray one another, and shall hate one another." (Matthew 24:10 KJV).

    b.   It's rather clear throughout the west today; there is a culture of political correctness that results in God's word not being preached because it is seen as offensive. Whether it's not politically correct or if it

causes a micro aggression, it seems that
The Bible is undesirable in the ears of those
who hate God and therefore hate one
another.

Who is Elijah

Elijah the Prophet came to us twice so far in the scripture. He is coming again a final and third time for a revival unlike anything we have seen. Elijah was a man who in the book of kings stood in the courts of the godless, the defiled, the wicked and he represented the light of the world, the light of the truth. Although he prayed that God would take his life as it would be easier, he chose to make the world a better place through decisive action by means of faith. Every day he walked with God and was taken to heaven without seeing death. John the Baptist was the Elijah during Jesus' day. Get ready for Elijah is coming, but who is he? Elijah has characteristics that are unique to him:

1. He is the messenger of The Covenant. (Malachi 3:1 KJV).
2. He said, I am the voice of one crying in the wilderness, Make straight the way of the Lord, as said the prophet Esaias. (John 1:23 KJV).
3. John the Baptist was considered Elijah. (Matthew 11:14 KJV).
4. He is associated with rain. (1 Kings 18:41 KJV).
5. He will be able to breathe fire against his enemies. (Revelation 11:5 KJV).
   a. The false prophet of Revelation will pretend to be Elijah by calling down fire from heaven. The Devil will make this lie a reality. (Revelation 13:13 KJV).
6. Just as John the Baptist closed out the Old Testament, modern day Elijah will close out most of The New Testament. This is known as the end of the church

age and the beginning of the millennial kingdom. (Malachi 3:1 KJV).

7. His message will focus on repentance and will be powerful. (Mark 1:4 KJV).
8. He will instruct kings and rulers. (1 Kings 18 KJV).
9. He will be the greatest prophet born of women. (Luke 7:28 KJV).
10. The third and last coming of Elijah will be associated with the following:
    a. Great wind, Earthquake, Fire
    b. Notice how these three things align with California. (1 Kings 19:11 KJV).
    c. Also, notice how when Elijah shows up in the New Testament, it is during The Transfiguration of Jesus Christ. This is during the feast of tabernacles which perfectly aligns with California's fire season.
    d. He will most likely be a king as it is written, "It is the glory of God to conceal a thing: but the honour of kings is to search out a matter." Proverbs 25:2 KJV. What happens if he searches for Jesus and finds him? Elijah speaks with God at the Transfiguration.

Warning to the Church

A great falling away was prophesized by Paul in 2 Thessalonians 2:1-3 KJV. "And because iniquity shall abound, the love of many shall wax cold." (Matthew 24:12 KJV). We were never meant to live this way. This world was meant to be a paradise. As it is written in Matthew 6:10 KJV, "Thy kingdom come, Thy will be done in earth as it is in heaven". Sin is what has made us lost, but we can be found.

With each passing generation, we continue to drift from biblical truth. Our churches are more impacted by worldliness, more distant from God. We have reached a point today where most youth believe that The Bible is only a set of good principles of how to be and act. There is very little belief in the omnipresence, miracles, and gifts of Jesus Christ. Therefore, many youth believe that you just pick a religion, any religion as if they are the same. Jesus said at The Tomb of Lazarus, "I am the resurrection, and the life: he that believeth in me, though he were dead, yet shall he live:" (John 11:25 KJV). There is only one way into heaven, and it's through Jesus Christ.

Many church leaders are like the Pharisees in Jesus' time. They teach others about Jesus Christ, yet they do not love him. They love their status, wealth, and power. For it is written, "Love not the world, neither the things that are in the world. If any man love the world, the love of the father is not in him." (1 John 2:15 KJV). The worldliness that has affected church leaders has driven false doctrines and practice into the church, they are as follows:

False Doctrine #1 The Cross was not sufficient for the remission of sins

Why is it that some church leadership categorizes sin and judges such sins as if they know their weight and distance from God? It is widely held that Mortal Sins keep us out of The Kingdom of Heaven, but this is not written in the scriptures. Doesn't this also mean that the cross was not enough for all sins if mortal sins keep us out of heaven unless forgiven by a priest? Also, why should church leaders judge which sins are mortal? We are commanded not to judge others for their sins. Wouldn't it be wise for us to not judge the weight of sins, therefore we cannot judge who is the worst sinner? Who are we to say which sins are not to worry about and which are grave? This seems like a very dark road to embark upon. It is written in Romans 2:1-2 KJV, "Therefore thou art inexcusable, O man, whosoever thou art that judgest: for wherein thou judgest another, thou condemnest thyself; for thou that judgest doest the same things. But we are sure that the judgement of God is according to truth against them which commit such things." Therefore is judgement by mankind an act against God? Shouldn't we let God judge for us? Another commonly held view is the narrative of Purgatory. Purgatory is a place where souls of the deceased go to purify themselves before going to Heaven. This purification isn't in the scripture, and does it not reaffirm the false narrative that the cross was not sufficient?

False Doctrine #2 Sunday as The Sabbath Day

Exodus 20:8-10 KJV, "Remember the Sabbath day, to keep it holy. Six days shall thou labour, and do all thy work: But the seventh day is the Sabbath of the Lord thy God: in it thou shalt not do any work, thou, nor thy son, nor thy daughter, thy manservant, nor thy maidservant, nor thy cattle, nor thy stranger that is within thy gates:" The seventh day in the Hebrew and Gregorian calendar is Saturday and not Sunday. How did we possibly make this error? The Saturday Sabbath is to celebrate when God stopped creating the world. Therefore The Sabbath being on Sunday is honoring the nothingness before creation.

"Come unto me, all ye that labour and are heavy laden, and I will give you rest." (Matthew 11:28 KJV). Believing in Jesus will provide our souls with rest every day of the week. The tiredness you feel that no amount of sleep can ever cure is the emptiness that can be removed through accepting Jesus and being born again. Therefore, the Sabbath truly has two parts.

False Doctrine #3 Calling Priests "Father"

Matthew 23:9 KJV, "And call no man your father upon the earth: for one is your Father, which is in heaven."

False Doctrine #4 Modifying the Bible and Additional Testaments

Revelation 22:19 KJV, "And if any man shall take away from the words of the book of this prophecy, God shall take away this part out of the book of life, and out of the holy city, and from the things which are written in this book." The entire Bible contains prophecy; therefore modification is condemning to those involved in such. This blasphemy against God and disrespect for his word is appalling. There are only two prophets acknowledged in The Bible for the times in which we live, which are known as God's Two Witnesses. Only they can speak for God and they will most certainly never modify the scripture. (Revelation 11:10 KJV).

False Doctrine #5 Praying to Saints and not to God

"But thou, when thou prayest, enter into thy closet, and when thou has shut thy door, pray to thy Father which is in secret; and thy Father which seeth in secret shall reward thee openly." (Matthew 6:6 KJV). Why would you settle to pray to anyone who isn't God? You do not need anyone to intercede as he currently sees and hears you. You act as if God is not with us. Jesus said, "Teaching them to observe all things whatsoever I have commanded you: and, lo, I am with you alway, even unto the end of the world. Amen." (Matthew 28:20 KJV).

Beware of praying to The Queen of Heaven. "The children gather wood, and the fathers kindle the fire, and the women knead their dough, to make cakes to the queen of heaven, and to pour out drink offerings unto other gods, that they may provoke me to anger. Do they provoke me to anger? saith the Lord: do they not provoke themselves to the confusion of their own faces? Therefore thus saith the Lord God; Behold, mine anger and my fury shall be poured out upon this place, upon man, and upon beast, and upon the trees of the field, and upon the fruit of the ground; and it shall burn, and shall not be quenched." (Jeremiah 7:18-20 KJV). The Queen of Heaven is a pagan reference to the goddess Ishtar. Mary is not The Queen of Heaven. Heaven has no queen. Almighty God, The King of Heaven, has no wife. That being said, we do have an obligation to honor the saints including Mary. However let us not confuse who we pray to or what titles we use.

False Doctrine #6 Prosperity Gospel

Forcing guilt upon your church members so that they will tithe is a disgrace. Teaching your audience that you will be far wealthier after they tithe is a lie. Building churches and megachurches for the purpose of wealth creation is evil. You love money more than God. Out of respect, you will not be called out by name as you know who you are. "And again I say to you, It is easier for a camel to go through the eye of a needle, than for a rich man to enter into the kingdom of God." (Matthew 19:24 KJV). Hoarding wealth is a sign of worldliness and loving money is a trait that is far from God. When it comes to giving, your congregation should speak the truth as much as possible everywhere they go before donating money. "Because you say, 'I am rich, have become wealthy, and have need of nothing'— and do not know that you are wretched, miserable, poor, blind, and naked..." (Revelation 3:17 KJV).

False Doctrine #7 Climate Change

Climate Change is a lie. Whether it's called man-made climate change or global dimming or global warming, these things are not done by means of pollution. Almighty God is in control of the weather. It is written, "That ye may be the children of your Father which is in heaven: for he maketh his sun to rise on the evil and on the good, and sendeth rain on the just and on the unjust." (Matthew 5:45 KJV). Not only does sin destroy the individual, but it has the capacity to destroy nations. "And I will make the land desolate, because they have committed a trespass, saith the Lord GOD." (Ezekiel 15:8 KJV). There is a solution to this so called climate crisis, which is really a sin crisis. It is written in 2 Chronicles 7:14 KJV, "If my people, which are called by my name, shall humble themselves, and pray, and seek my face, and turn from their wicked ways; then will I hear from heaven, and will forgive their sin, and will heal their land." We do know that we have a responsibility to take care of this planet as God will destroy those who destroy the earth. (Revelation 11:18 KJV). What is troubling is that our religious leadership either doesn't know what is written in The Bible, or they do not care. Which is worse? Do not allow the totalitarian politicians and religious leaders control over how we live, our relationship to God, and our very destiny.

False Doctrine #8 Replacement Theology

The narrative that The Children of Israel are no longer God's chosen people is anti-Semitic. They will always be God's chosen people. Also, who is to say that The Old Testament is no longer valid or true? The Old and New Testament are both true and always will be. This hateful anti-Semitic ideology is evil and unbiblical. For God said to Abram, "I will bless those who bless you, And I will curse him who curses you; And in you all the families of the earth shall be blessed." (Genesis 12:3 KJV). The Jewish people will always be blessed by God. In addition, the coming signs and wonders of revelation will perfectly tie in Old Testament wonders for the purpose of salvation of The Jewish People. Israel will know that Jesus Christ is Lord. For it is written, "And so all Israel shall be saved: as it is written, There shall come out of Sion the Deliverer, and shall turn away ungodliness from Jacob:" (Romans 11:26 KJV).

False Doctrine #9 Wrath without Love

Jesus Christ perfectly balances wrath, love, and redemption. Many have heard of God's anger for their sins. How their deeds are evil. Have those same people ever heard of God's love or how to be redeemed? The distance between God and yourself can be closed if you deny yourself and pick up your cross and follow Jesus Christ. It is written in Exodus 20:5 KJV that God is jealous. He is jealous because he wants a relationship with you. Always remember, "But without faith it is impossible to please him: for he that cometh to God must believe that he is, and that he is a rewarder of them that diligently seek him." (Hebrews 11:6 KJV).

False Doctrine #10 Alliance with the Wicked

We have a duty to love our enemies and those who do not believe, but we should never make an alliance with those who do not believe in Jesus Christ. "Be ye not unequally yoked together with unbelievers: for what fellowship hath righteousness with unrighteousness? And what communion hath light with darkness?" (2 Corinthians 6:14 KJV). In addition, God commands us to not intermarry with nonbelievers in Deuteronomy 7:3-5 KJV. When politicians and religious leaders say that we all worship the same god, it is not true. If you do not accept Jesus Christ, prepare for an eternity in everlasting fire. Do not appease the unbeliever, make no pact with them, and do not push an idea that we all worship the same god. To be precise, The God of Israel and Jesus Christ are the same.

False Doctrine #11 Jesus and The Father are not the same

"I and my Father are one." (John 10:30 KJV). "Jesus said unto them, Verily, verily, I say unto you, Before Abraham was, I am." (John 8:58 KJV).

False Doctrine #12 The Messiah never came to Earth

God promised us through The Prophet Isaiah that our Lord would be harmed for our sake. "But he was wounded for our transgressions, he was bruised for our iniquities: the chastisement of our peace was upon him; and with his stripes we are healed." (Isaiah 53:5 KJV). God tells us that the Messiah will be born in Bethlehem through Micah, "But thou, Bethlehem Ephratah, though thou be little among the thousands of Judah, yet out of thee shall he come forth unto me that is to be ruler in Israel; whose goings forth have been from of old, from everlasting." (Micah 5:2 KJV). The scripture also says that he will be the peace when the Assyrian comes into The Holy Land in Micah 5:5 KJV. Therefore by all of this, we can determine that he came to save us from sin and is coming again to save us from The Assyrian. Our savior's name is Jesus Christ.

The Church Going Forward

We as The Church of Jesus Christ can resolve our shortcomings and realign ourselves to Jesus if we:

1. Place The Bible as the supreme authority in our churches instead of human leadership
2. Guard our hearts against the enemy and ensure that only Jesus lives in us
3. Consistently speak the truth and continue to pursue Jesus

Just as in Jesus' time, his people were lost and sin was rampant. Remember the promises of Jesus and what is to come. Just as he promised, "And Jesus answered and said unto them, Elias truly shall first come, and restore all things." (Matthew 17:11 KJV). Understand the season that we are in my friends, the greatest revival the world has ever seen is coming. "And in the morning, It will be foul weather to day: for the sky is red and lowring. O ye hypocrites, ye can discern the face of the sky; but can ye not discern the signs of the time?"(Matthew 16:3 KJV). When this revival begins, it will require average people to do their part as well.

Outro

A great Christian revival is coming and it will impact the entire world. Everything is about to change. Therefore as a result of duty and goodwill, this work has been written to inform many with regards to the most important dream anyone could ever have, **To find and be worthy of Jesus Christ's eternal presence**. We have an obligation to pursue this dream while attempting to perfect our relationship with Jesus Christ.

To provide some examples of what can be understood as a result of seeking and finding:

1. A great Christian Revival will begin in California in the near future. It will rain during a wildfire when great numbers of people begin to pray for forgiveness and turn from their sins.
2. Donald Trump claiming victory for a second term due to a biblical parallel with King David.
3. Jesus Christ will finally be famous in every street in the west, as it once was.

What happens when every man has established a relationship with Jesus Christ and perfected it? What actions must we take as a society? What actions must we take when we make our hearts pure? What then becomes our responsibility? For unto whomsoever much is given, of him shall be much required.

Always remember that it is God who raises up kings. "It is the glory of God to conceal a thing: but the honour of kings is to search out a matter." (Proverbs 25:2 KJV). Even in the 21st century, God can raise up a royal family that will lead The Church and defend Israel. When this happens, all shall know that these things are done by Jesus Christ.

Reference

Christian Art Publishers. (2017). KJV Budget Softcover Gold. New York, United States: Macmillan Publishers.

Made in the USA
Monee, IL
02 September 2020

JOE: Look, just try to relax a little. You need to relax.

AMANDA: How can I relax with a prehistoric monster in your bathroom and two men following me? Did you wash your hands?

JOE: I thought you said one guy was following you.

AMANDA: I don't know. *(Amanda sits on the floor and frantically digs around in her purse for a cigarette.)*

JOE: You're a good-looking girl. What's your name?

AMANDA: *(Looking him over suspiciously.)* My name is . . . Marge. Yeah . . . my name is Marge. *(Amanda continues to dig frantically in her purse. She retrieves a cigarette and continues to dig for a match.)* Do you have a light?

JOE: Oh, now Marge . . . You shouldn't be smoking. It's not good for you.

AMANDA: Look . . . Oh, never mind.

JOE: What's your old man's name?

AMANDA: Who?

JOE: The dude who has your key. What's his name?

AMANDA: Oh . . . his name. *(She thinks for a second.)* Uhhh . . . Joe.

JOE: Joe! You're kidding. My name is Joe!

(A loud thudding noise comes from the bathroom. Amanda and Joe both scream and grab each other.)

JOE: Now calm down! You have got to calm down! You're going to upset Amanda again.

AMANDA: Amanda . . . who's Amanda?

JOE: My snake.

AMANDA: You mean that thing lives here?

(Amanda breaks loose from Joe, quickly crosses to the window and looks out, then back to the door and looks through the peephole.)

AMANDA: I think I'll just go now. Maybe I'll see you around. By the way, my Joe is a cop slash detective and is really experienced in that karate stuff. As a matter of fact, he's right now practicing to be a Navy Seal . . . while he's in jail. Yep . . . he's in jail. He'll be out today. He killed two people. He was there for killing two people . . . in cold blood. See ya. *(Amanda exits, backing out the door.)*

ARMADILLO

(2 males/2 females, comedy)

BREAKDOWN Two old friends, Marge and Sharon, meet at a bar. Marge has just been fired; Sharon is in her last month of pregnancy.

SETTING A popular, dimly lit bar in Manhattan.

• • •

(Sharon is sitting at a bar alone, sipping her drink. She looks at her watch, then puts on her coat and takes one last sip when Marge enters.)

MARGE: Hi. Thanks for meeting me. I hope I didn't keep you waiting too long. Wow, you look great! How do you feel?

SHARON: Really good. I walked all the way from 81st Street . . . It's OK, the doctor said walking was good for me. Now you . . . you sounded so upset. How are you? Are you going to be OK?

MARGE: No! Yeah. No! Actually, I hate him! I know I came across like a good sport after he fired me. But the truth is I hate his guts. I hope he . . . I hope he . . . I hope he loses all his money! No worse . . . I hope he loses all his poofy, puffy hair!

SHARON: *(Laughs.)* You came across great, and he shouldn't have fired you! You were the best project manager they had!

MARGE: I know, but I still can't believe it! What are you drinking? Bartender, straight Tequila, a shot—make it a double. What are you having?

SHARON: Tea. Doctor's orders . . . and no, I don't mind.

MARGE: I felt like such a fool—a total loser. You saw the other girls ganging up on me—especially that one bitch . . . I mean totally. ME, head of . . .

(The bartender hands her, her drink.)

MARGE: Oh, thanks. *(Marge takes her drink, does the salt, the lime, downs the Tequila, and continues to talk.)* What was I saying?

SHARON: Head of your class at Yale . . . a Rhodes Scholar . . . magnum cum laude . . . junior partner of the biggest law firm in New York, etc., etc.

(Marge waves to the bartender.)

MARGE: Another shot—make it a triple!

SHARON; Whoa, you gonna be OK?

MARGE: Don't forget—nobody can outdrink me either! God! I hate him! "Marge—you're fired!" I will hear those words forever. What a nightmare. I'll never be able to face . . . *(Marge notices Jim and Tad entering the bar.)* ON NO! OHHH NO! Look who's coming.

(Sharon looks.)

MARGE: Don't look! Oh, it's too late.

(Jim and Tad walk over to Marge and Sharon. The men are drunk.)

MARGE: *(Sweetly.)* Hiii!

JIM: Hey!

TAD: How are you doing?

MARGE: Great! Oh, meet my friend, Sharon.

SHARON: Hello.

(Both men zoom in on Sharon.)

JIM: Heey.

TAD: How's it going?

SHARON: I'm good, thank you.

JIM: *(To Marge.)* You're a class act! You did great!

MARGE: Thanks—you're prejudiced.

JIM: No, really, you were great. What are you drinking?

MARGE: Tequila—and I'll have just one more eensy-teensy-weensy shot. Bartender . . .

SHARON: Are you sure?

MARGE: Sure. I've got my car. You can be the designated driver. Bartender, another shot. *(Marge holds up three fingers.)*

JIM: Hey, let's celebrate. A round for us . . . and the pretty ladies. Doubles?

TAD: Triples! *(Tad stumbles and falls on the floor disappearing behind the barstools. They all laugh. Tad pulls himself up to a barstool.)* I'm cool . . . I'm cool . . . It's all good. I can handle it. A TOAST! . . . Screw Trump! And his towers!

JIM: HERE! HERE! To beauty and brains!

(Tad to Sharon.)

TAD: To . . . ?

SHARON: Sharon.

TAD: SHARON!

TAD: And that chick, Armadillo . . . what a cooold bitch . . .

MARGE: Esmeralda.

SHARON: Amarosa.

TAD: A TOAST! Here's to . . . Ama . . . Arma . . . .

SHARON: Amarosa.

TAD: AMAROSA! *(Tad falls down on the floor again, and they all laugh.)*

SHARON: *(Grimacing in pain.)* OOOOhhh.

(Tad struggles back up to his chair. Marge and Jim are singing.)

TAD: What was that?

JIM: I don't know.

SHARON: *(Louder.)* OOOOOHHHHH!

(They all look at Sharon and freeze.)

MARGE: OH NO!

SHARON: It's time!

JIM: Time for what?!

TAD: Another toast!

MARGE: NO! She's having a baby!

SHARON: OOOOOOOOHHHHHH! *(Breathing short breaths,)*

TAD: OH . . . UH . . . What are we suppose to do?

JIM: I don't know.

MARGE: Bartender, HELP! Call a taxi!

TAD: No! Call the fire department! I saw that on *E.R.* They always call the fire department. Here's to the FIRE DEPARTMENT!

JIM: HERE! HERE!

SHARON: OOOOHHHH!

MARGE: Honey, just hold on, relax! Hold my hand! BREATHE!

TAD: Somebody boil some water! Why do they always say that in the movies?

JIM: I don't know.

MARGE: Be serious!!

TAD: If it's a girl, don't name her Armadillo!

JIM: HERE! HERE!

(Jim and Tad laugh.)

MARGE: I said be serious! Breathe, honey, breathe! And if it's a boy, don't name him Donald.

BEST FRIENDS

(2 males/1 female, drama)

BREAKDOWN   Sonny and Norma Jean have been best friends since childhood. He is secretly in love with her.
SETTING   A small town in Texas, in the garage at Sonny's house.

• • •

(Sonny is in his garage repairing an old ice-cream maker. There is a radio playing some Chris Isaak music in the background. Norma Jean, dressed provocatively and barefoot, tiptoes up behind Sonny and puts her hands over his eyes. She speaks with a sultry, long, drawn-out Texas accent.)

NORMA JEAN: Hi.

SONNY: Oh, hi. I didn't hear you come in.

NORMA JEAN: What are you doin' there?

SONNY: Oh, not much . . . just piddlin' around.

NORMA JEAN: Looks like a pretty old ice-cream maker.

SONNY: Yeah, but it's just about to get put back together.

NORMA JEAN: You sure are good at that kind of stuff. You wanna come over later . . . for some ice tea . . . or somethin'?

(There is a pause as Sonny looks her over.)

SONNY: Now, whaddya think you're up to? Huh? Where's Tony?

NORMA JEAN: Now, don't look at me like that. And I don't care where Tony is. Anyway, you know where he is. He's out with that slut. He don't care nothin' about me or the baby . . . Look,

I don't want to be by myself all night. You could come over for a little while, couldn't you? Please. He's gonna be out all night.

SONNY: No, I'm not gonna let you get yourself into hot water with him. He's crazy. I don't even know how you got hooked up with him.

NORMA JEAN: I just need you to hold me. I've been through a real hard time since Mama died. She was always there for me. I could talk to her.

SONNY: You're still a little girl, aren't you . . . missin' your mama. I don't blame you. She was a good woman. I miss her, too. I'm sorry you don't have her now . . . but she's in a . . .

NORMA JEAN: Please, come over tonight . . . just for a little while. I'm gonna be stuck there all night long all by myself with the baby. I just can't bear it.

(Sonny digs into his pocket and takes out a small gold ring with a ruby in it and looks at it.)

SONNY: I want you to have this.

NORMA JEAN: Why that's beautiful! How come you're giving it to me? Where'd you get it?

SONNY: It was my grandma Lucy's. I found it in one of her dresser drawers when we sold her house. I've carried it around with me ever since for good luck and to remind me of her. Here . . . you take it now.

NORMA JEAN: Oh, I just couldn't.

SONNY: Please . . . I bet it'll make you feel a lot better right now, even better than a hug.

NORMA JEAN: No, I just couldn't.

(Sonny takes her hand and slides the ring on her finger. Norma Jean puts her arms around Sonny and gives him a good hug. He hugs her back.)

SONNY: You sure are a pretty little thing, and you got a good heart. Why do you take that from Tony?

NORMA JEAN: He used to be nice.

(Suddenly a car drives up and screeches to a halt. Tony jumps out.)

TONY: What are you doing here? And you, punk, get your hands off my wife.

NORMA JEAN: Oh, Tony, just go away. We were just sittin' here and you know it.

TONY: Shut up, bitch!

SONNY: Hey, don't talk to her that way!

TONY: I said get away from my wife, punk.

SONNY: Look, nothin' was going on here. You're drunk. Now let her alone. She's having a hard time over her mother . . . in case you haven't noticed.

TONY: And what do you know about my wife?

NORMA JEAN: Tony, just shut up! Where's your slut? Huh? Just go back to your slut!

TONY: You're the only slut around here!

SONNY: Hey, now back off. You're drunk and I don't want to hurt you.

TONY: *(Laughing.)* Oh, a real tough guy. I'm reeeal scared.

SONNY: I'm warning you. You don't want any trouble from me.

(Tony grabs Norma Jean by the hair, pulls her over to him, takes out a knife, and holds it to her throat.)

TONY: Now you shut up or I'll slit her throat. And if I ever see you around her again, I'll cut your guts out. Now she's coming with me. I've got some business with her.

SONNY: OK . . . take it easy. Now, just calm down. You don't really want to hurt her. C'mon now, just let her go.

NORMA JEAN: Tony, let go of me! You're hurting me!

(Sonny goes to take the knife from Tony, and Tony shoves it into Sonny's stomach. Norma Jean screams. Sonny backs up. He has both his hands around the handle of the knife. He drops to his knees and falls forward. Tony runs to his car and takes off. Norma Jean drops to her knees and wraps her arms around Sonny.)

NORMA JEAN: Sonny! Sonny! Oh, my God, somebody help us! Please help us! Sonny, don't die, please. Sonny, don't die. I love you, Sonny. Please don't die.

CASTING CALL

(1 male/1 female, romance)

BREAKDOWN Debbie and Sean are auditioning for a television series that is being kept confidential. Sean has already been cast in the lead role. The studio is using a scene from *The Newlanders* to audition the actors.

SETTING A casting office at Paramount Pictures.

• • •

SEAN: I'm coming *meine Dame.* I'm coming!

DEBBIE: I demand to be returned to the ship. I will not get back on that godforsaken wagon! You have had more than enough time to find Gottleib's cousin, or whoever he is. You are more interested in selling those unfortunate people you have chained up like monkeys.

SEAN: *Meine Dame*, it is Sunday. I can do nothing today. All the bureaus are closed.

DEBBIE: They were not closed yesterday!

SEAN: *(Pleading.)* I am working as fast as I can. Please be patient.

DEBBIE: *(Demanding.)* Take me to the ship! I wish to be with my children. We will wait onboard for Gottlieg. The ship might have arrived already.

SEAN: *(Threatening.)* It is quite impossible, *meine Dame.* I must ask you to quiet down, or I shall have to take measures to see that you do.

(Debbie grabs Sean's shirt with her left hand while faking a hard slap with her right hand. Sean stumbles backward against the wall.)